CW01391710

EVOKE

NINA MAGON

WRITTEN WITH JILL SIERACKI

DEDICATED TO
MY FAMILY, FRIENDS, SUPPORTERS, CLIENTS, AND, MOST IMPORTANTLY, TO ALL THE DREAMERS.

THE ROUTE to Delhi was never the same. Growing up in

Canada, my family would frequently return to India and with every passage, we would travel a different course, visiting the world's most culturally significant cities. Those dramatic detours profoundly impacted my global approach to design and shaped the award-winning practice I steer today.

Throughout my career, I have taken the time to meticulously craft inspired interiors that offer a passport into some of the world's most captivating destinations, combining modern elements with custom creations to transportive effect. For a "Contessa's Bedroom" in a South Florida show house, I blended unexpected materials, fashion-forward contemporary artwork, and ethereal elements to create a sexy suite that conjures the feeling of a romantic sojourn in Milan. For a luxury jeweler in Texas, I designed an upscale lounge with European allure, bringing together striking architectural details with sumptuous textiles. Through my global lens, a decadent spa in Houston was utterly transformed using the vibrant colors of the Mediterranean. My residential and commercial interiors are powerful, style-setting, and I hope, truly unforgettable.

More importantly, each of these spaces is timeless, a word that is frequently bandied about in our industry to denote an interior that offers no cues to when it was created. I prefer to view timelessness from a different angle; I gravitate more toward the idea that the beauty and majesty of a room endures long after it was first revealed, even if nothing has changed. Landmarks that inspire design connoisseurs to visit, almost like pilgrimages, such as the Taj Mahal in Agra, India, France's Palace of Versailles, or Villa Necchi Campiglio in Milan, have stood for ages without a single edit, and I can't fathom a viewer who would take in their grandeur and proclaim, "Time for an update!" Their breathtaking details, many of which incorporate popular adornments of the period they were first installed, still astonish—and will continue to do so for eons to come.

With this book, I hope to leave you with an unbridled sense of wanderlust and arouse a spirit of awe and wonderment. With a careful balance of high-gloss modernism and old-world grandeur, eye-catching furnishings that define a room and artfully conceived accents that gently make their presence known, every interior I design should be approached with a sensation of discovery, allowing a slow reveal of its decadent details. I hope you find something new and tantalizing each time you turn a page.

Each project starts like that road map to Delhi—with paths branching off in infinite possibilities and every turn pushing the conversation forward in an exciting new direction. My interiors channel the striking details of a cosmopolitan city, culling inspiration from towers of glass and steel, and incorporate the patina of an ancient village into a seductive space composed of thoughtful layers. I have translated the palettes and materials that captured my own imagination in Sicily, Santorini, Mykonos, Istanbul, and Paris into homes as close as Houston and as far as Abu Dhabi.

Whether you are a jet-setter or homebody, I hope you will be taken by the intoxicating sense of possibility each of these interiors offers. So what are you waiting for? Let the journey begin . . .

IMAGINE

Whether implemented in a minimalist palette or deployed in a full spectrum of hues, color can radically affect the mood of any room.

CERTAIN cities have come to be defined as much by their color palette

as they are by their architectural style: Venetian red on the palazzi that front the Grand Canal, the terra-cotta facades of Tuscany's rustic villas, the creamy beige of Paris's limestone buildings. But perhaps no color combination is more synonymous with a place than the crisp white and cobalt blue that envelop the picturesque city of Santorini. Amidst the Cycladic island's limewashed homes, free from palaver, the landscape practically reverberates with their snowy exteriors juxtaposed against a cloudless blue sky and turquoise Aegean Sea.

In design, color is one of the most powerful tools in our arsenal. By altering a color, you can radically shift the mood of a room, and selecting just the right saturation can be the most delicate balancing act. (To illustrate, imagine a pink interior. If you formulate a shade that's not too dark, not too light, not to red, not too vibrant, you get India Mahdavi's iconic Sketch restaurant in London; choose wrong and you're in Barbie's Dreamhouse.) The signature color of my firm, peacock green, to me means opulence and luxury; in Indian culture, it's a sign of wealth. In some installations, it can be serene and slightly mysterious, in others, uplifting and rejuvenating.

For a spacious residence in one of Houston's most desirable neighborhoods, I looked to the colors of the famed Grecian isles to compose a well-appointed home that gracefully walks the line between traditional and contemporary with softer, more muted moments contrasting rich, jewel-tone components.

Soft white walls with a textured plaster finish inspired by the vernacular of Santorini enveloped the entire interior in a tranquil beauty. Then, we layered in art, furniture, and other materials that echo those ethereal neutral hues, but with more contemporary shapes, giving the space its modern notes. In the entryway, a custom console of richly veined marble is paired with two romantic lighting installations of playful white blooms on the vine. An oversize artwork of dimensional cream-colored flowers anchors the dining room that supports a Lindsey Adelman branch chandelier with milky bubbles. Gauzy, cloudlike light fixtures dance above the living room, while a grand expanse of white stone anchors the kitchen island.

Then, like those picturesque roofs of Santorini, we added dramatic spots of color, most notably a cascade of globes in aquatic shades of peacock green, cobalt blue, turquoise, and amber that float like raindrops amid a curvaceous grand staircase. Jewel-tone seating in modern shapes from Roche Bobois, B&B Italia, and Paola Lenti share space with metallic accents and a striking Lucite billiards table. Giving the home warmth and texture are various wood elements—from wide-plank flooring and weathered ceiling beams to reclaimed pieces that front the kitchen island. Stone walls that appear as if formed in antiquity punctuate the powder room and kitchen, the latter where glass and blackened steel cabinets and pendants add a sophisticated new dimension.

While the palette for this home is conservative in its scope, it's powerful in its implementation, and by creatively using just a few carefully selected colors, we've crafted a cohesive interior imbued with harmony and authenticity. Less can often be more—whether that's a color plan for an interior design, a fantasy little black dress, or a postcard-perfect village overlooking one of the world's most beautiful ocean vistas.

In a stunning, design-forward home in Houston, a billowing Campana Brothers sofa and Tokujin Yoshioka stool from Louis Vuitton's Objets Nomades collection define this artful entryway punctuated by a romantic custom lighting installation.

While silky plaster envelops many of the rooms,
the kitchen features textural walls of rough-hewn
stone, adding to the space's old-world grandeur.

A shapely B&B Italia chair, upholstered in a rich plummy
fabric, connects to the other jewel tones in the space,
including the mixed-material Konekt stools and twelve
wine-colored seats in the adjoining dining room.

In the living room, the expansive back-to-back sofas
were selected over a narrower tête-à-tête couch,
offering plush seating areas for larger gatherings.

In the powder room, a feature wall of exposed brick and stucco creates a rugged backdrop for an unexpected light fixture of delicate clear glass and industrial elements.

A crescent-shaped Baxter sofa hugs the rounded curve of the brand's circular tables, one made using rose-colored stone and the other mixed metals, set upon a playful Kyle Bunting rug.

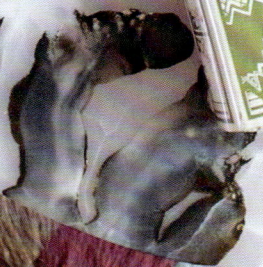

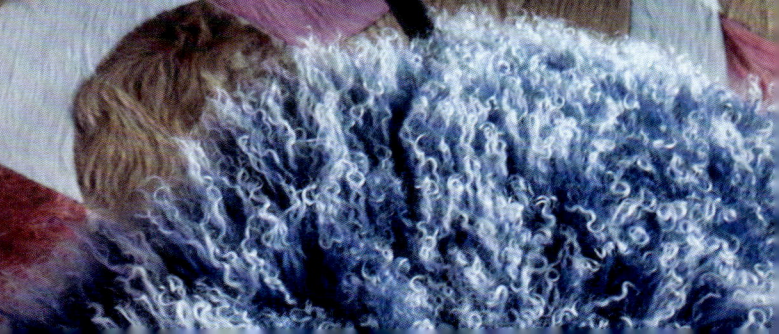

These debonair chaise longues, accessorized with
a Hermès throw, provide a sartorial spot for viewin

The terrace's stone fireplace and column coupled with a
selection of modern furnishings connect to the interior's
Cycladic palette of earthy neutrals and punctuating blues.

"COLOR IS THE VISUAL CUE THAT LEADS US ON AN EMOTIONAL JOURNEY, HEIGHTENING PASSION OR DRAWING US IN FOR A RESTORATIVE BREATH."

The monochromatic design plan for our CW Residence carries
through to the main bedroom, where a gestural abstract
surmounts a sumptuous bed dressed in crisp white linens.

An oversize cobalt-blue sectional from Paola Lenti adds energy to the residence's main living area, which is otherwise dressed in neutral shades of black, white, and heather gray.

"COLOR ALLOWS US TO PUSH THE BOUNDARIES OF PERCEPTION, CREATING AN OPTICAL ILLUSION THAT TANTALIZES THE IMAGINATION AND FORCES US TO RECONSIDER ALL THAT IS POSSIBLE."

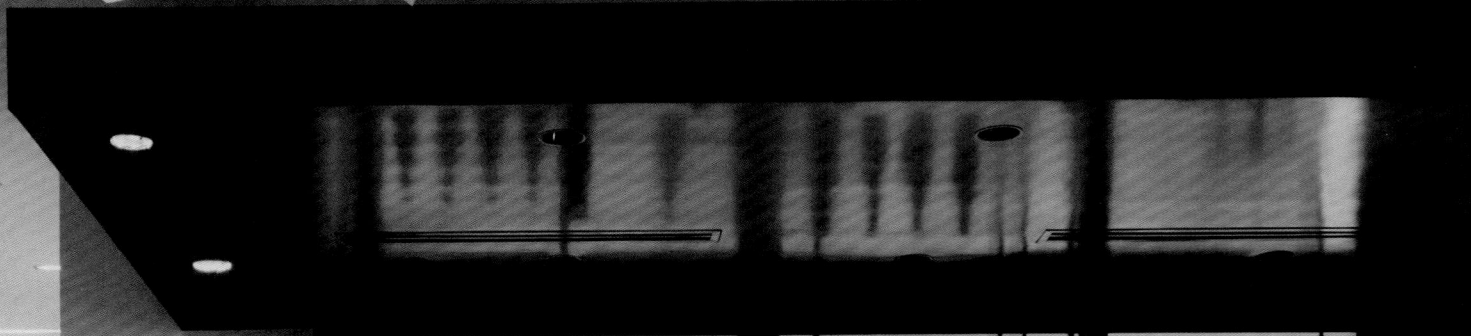

At Houston restaurant 51fifteen, wispy hexagons in the watercolor-like rug echo the honeycomb installation that stretches across the ceiling and down one wall set with Dekton by Cosentino. This project was the first and largest Dekton installation in North America.

A gleaming brass framework displays various bottles of champagne and other high-end spirits at 51 fifteen's satellite gathering place, Bar 12.

AWAKEN

Meticulously executed
architectural forms
can dramatically impact
a structure's exterior
but can be equally
striking when reimagined
on a smaller scale
in an interior design.

PERHAPS

no edifice in the world is as recognizable as Rome's Colosseum, its tiers of precisely executed arches distinguishing the structure as one of the finest examples of architecture ever created. Not only do the forms serve an engineering function, distributing the weight of the massive structure, they also provide an aesthetic tool, carving the facade into sculptural recesses with military precision. It's a design cue found repeatedly in significant landmarks around the world, from the Pont du Gard aqueduct in France to the Al-Aqsa Mosque in Jerusalem.

I leaned into the same Piranesian principles when composing the jewel box Nina Magon Lounge at preeminent Texas jeweler Zadok, visually lifting the ceiling with an artful installation of arches, configured in a Mondrian-like pattern. In a series of floor-to-ceiling styles, punctuated with a minimalist light fixture of my own design, an installation of Cosentino's magma-like Liquid Embers finish creates visual interest with contrasting color and an arresting mix of matte and gloss. In other recesses, mirrors carry the decor into new dimensions, reflecting the space's curated elements almost like abstract artworks—a string of pearl globes from my Studio M lighting collection here, a segment of the exterior's gold diamond-pattern grillwork there.

However, the room's most captivating optical illusion was reserved for the ceiling, where an expanse of hammered metal adds an otherworldly effect, the fractal panel bouncing natural light throughout the space and conjuring the illusion of looking up through crystal clear Mediterranean water.

Rounded edges serve as a through line in the lounge, from the multidimensional bar to a peacock-colored plaster finish suggesting patina to the circular cocktail tables and rug. Custom sofas, capsule-shaped chairbacks, and Jean Royère–inspired armchairs all follow the same melody, their soft forms contributing to the interior's flow, opening channels for visitors to effortlessly roam throughout. Dressed in our firm's signature shade of green, the lounge delivers opulence and luxury with global resonance much closer to home.

WORLD
OF
MAGON

The gold seen in the exterior grillwork is echoed in interior accents, like these Sophia dining chairs from my Pavus Collection, upholstered in our studio's signature shade of peacock green.

A welcoming space for Zadok's VIP clients, the lounge
also serves as a place for intimate private events.
The sinuous Ocelli sofas and tactile Pelosa chairs offer
seductive seating options for evening cocktails.

Balancing all the soft materials in the Nina Magon Lounge are painterly stones from Cosentino, inset in the collection of wall niches and sculpted into visually compelling table bases.

"FROM TOWERING AND MAJESTIC ARCHES TO A COLLECTED TABLEAU OF DECORATIVE FORMS, ARCHITECTURAL SHAPES HAVE THE POWER TO ELEVATE, CAPTIVATE, AND INSPIRE."

A mix of materials and periods inside our CC Residence project adds to the visual interest, including in this elegant living room, where blush-colored barrel chairs and a neutral sofa contrast with the ornate vintage high-back chair next to the fireplace.

An atmospheric wallcovering from Phillip Jeffries that suggests a misty stroll through a thick cover of weeping willow branches complements a dreamy dining room chandelier by John-Richard.

The residence's neutral kitchen is transformed with an inspired
mix of materials: crisp, cool metal on the range hood
is juxtaposed against sumptuous upholstery on the counter
stools and warm woods on the floor and ceiling.

In the primary bedroom, the smoky gray tones of shagreen side tables, enveloping armchairs, and restful bed linens are carried up to a ceiling installation that backs a luminous chandelier of iridescent glass.

In the primary bedroom,
the smoky gray tones of
shagreen side tables,
enveloping armchairs, and
restful bed linens are carried
up to a ceiling installation
that backs a luminous
chandelier of iridescent glass.

IMMERSE

While paying homage to history and tradition can take many forms, drawing on classic colors, natural materials, and recognizable textures can contribute to a cohesive, elevated interior.

FROM

New York to Los Angeles, Monaco to Mexico, newly introduced luxury spas often feature neutral palettes and natural woods, their austerity synonymous with today's idea of tranquility and zen. Unswayed by trend, I find myself drawn to the more historical landmarks like the Széchenyi thermal baths in Budapest or the Friedrichsbad spa in Baden-Baden, Germany—icons of wellness that endure as architectural marvels, with towering Corinthian and Ionic columns, soaring cupolas, and frescoes surrounding healing waters that have been community gathering spots for centuries.

For the Solaya Spa & Salon in Houston, I wanted to translate that historic vernacular into a contemporary setting, elevating a modern destination with thoughtful elements rich with patina. Mirrored metal doors, aged into a gorgeous verdigris hue, lead guests into the spa, where oversize antique double doors, covered in expressive carvings, look as if they were plucked directly from a hôtel particulier in Paris's 6th arrondissement, then installed here to imbue the space with grandeur.

In revamping the spa, we reconfigured the layout, letting the interior breathe, and reimagined the herringbone floors in a more layered honey-blonde hue, its multitude of shades infusing the space with an added dimension and character. Refractive installations, such as two wall hangings composed of droplet-shaped Murano glass bulbs and ornate antique chandeliers of faceted crystal, discovered animating castles in Europe, add to the airiness, bouncing the desirable natural light throughout Solaya's lounge and service areas.

Furthering the romance of the spa is the space's plethora of rounded edges—from newly formed carved recesses in the ceiling to the sinuous hallway I wrapped in a Wall&decò wallpaper featuring a soft, water-color-like mural of robust blossoms. An oblong chaise paired with a cylindrical side table and a circular rug sit in conversation with the modern capsular form of the reception desk.

Apothecary shelves that channel the old-world splendor of Florence's famed Santa Maria Novella pharmacy take on a more elegant repertoire when painted a saturated shade of peacock green and backed in a luxurious natural stone, its wispy veins echoed in a complementary marble table. With a palette drawing influence from the healing waters that have lured wellness seekers for centuries and a selection of profound details thoughtfully considered to invoke serenity, Solaya's final design enveloped guests in a spirit of quietude and relaxation just steps from the hustle and bustle of Houston.

An antique chandelier of faceted crystal hangs from a ceiling recess lined with Wall&decò's Niveum wallcovering at Houston's Solaya Spa & Salon.

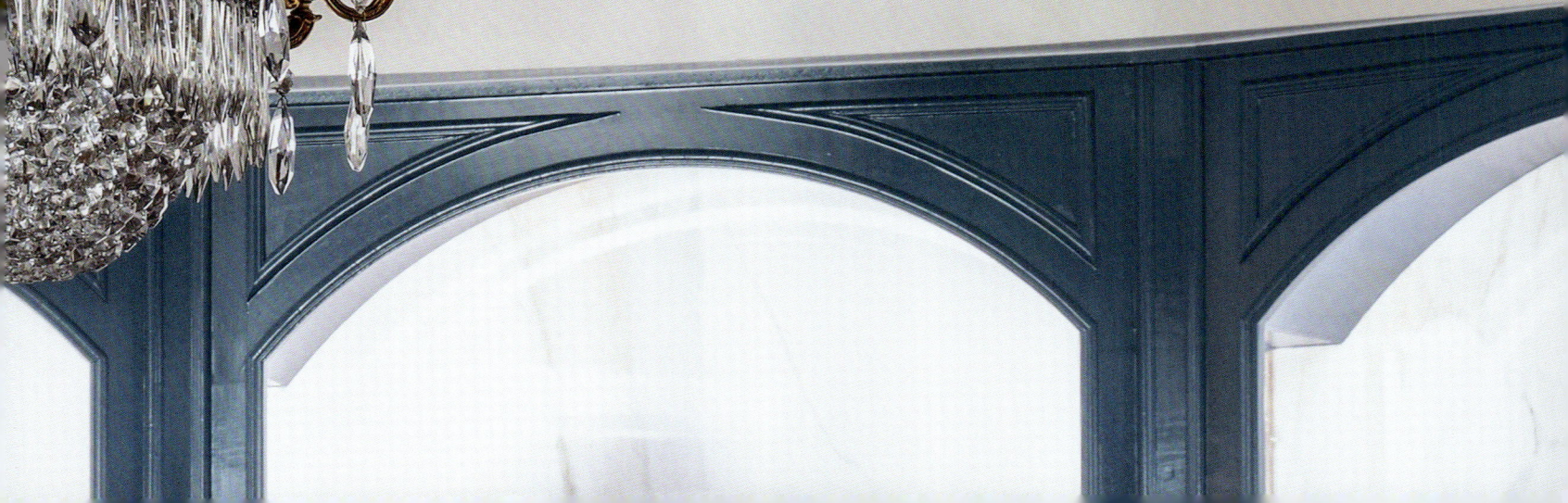

Adding to the space's air of classicism are the elegant herringbone
floors that connect the newly installed capsular desk with an artfully
composed seating area of curvaceous sofas and circular tables.

Ornate doors infuse the space with an air of
old-world grandeur while the oblong table, chic
velvet chairs, and wall installations of Murano glass
droplets balance the design with modern elements.

Creamy white walls and honey-blonde flooring contribute to the spa's
soothing atmosphere while case goods and seating in the
studio's signature peacock hue offer notes of luxury and sophistication.

"TO CARESS THE SURFACE OF A MATERIAL IS TO EXPERIENCE ITS ESSENCE AND CONNECT WITH ITS HISTORY, ITS BEAUTY ITS INTRIGUE."

To boost the sense of harmony in this Houston home our HW Residence, we called in an expert or Vastu Shastra, a traditional Indian practice similar to feng shui, who collaborated with our team to improve the flow of energy throughout the interior design

Columns and millwork were completely
transformed using a single shade of crisp white
that reinvigorated the HW Residence's interior
with an overall brightness and sense of airiness.

Large floor tiles lend a minimalist look to the main bath while a feature wall outfitted in Dekton Stonika Bergen gives a spa-like background to a contemporary freestanding Kohler tub.

A monochromatic bedroom maintains a feeling of peacefulness while still allowing for high design, including a dramatic B&B Italia bed, modern KDLN pendants, and graceful Gallotti&Radice side tables.

"THE INTERPLAY OF LIGHT AND SHADOW IS THE MOST INTOXICATING DANCE IN DESIGN AS ELEMENTS OF A ROOM GLIDE INTO THE FOREFRONT OR RETREAT TO QUIET CORNERS."

A bedroom in the G Residence, in Houston's Giorgetti residential complex, benefits from an Élitis wallpaper backdrop that mirrors the restful colors carried through to the Minotti chairs and painterly rug from London Grey Rugs.

Rich details such as the dashingly composed shelves, wall installation by Moderno Porcelain Works, and selection of Minotti furnishings elevate this cozy gathering area.

Clear glass orbs allow this magnificent Gallotti&Radice chandelier to almost disappear during the day. At night, it casts a seductive glow over the brand's Platium table set with sartorial Giorgetti dining chairs.

PASSION

Not always for the faint of heart, pink is bold; it has the power to seduce with romantic shades and uplift with rosy interpretations.

BEFORE
there was Herb Ritts, Helmut Newton, or even Irving Penn, there was Horst P. Horst, whose surrealist fashion photographs graced the covers of French, British, and eventually American *Vogue*. Capturing icons of stage and screen, he photographed with cinematic quality the high-society swans of the era, situating them in innocently seductive poses against moody backdrops or architectural forms. It was a Horst P. Horst image that inspired one of my most recognized rooms.

Participating in a show house can be an intense experience for a designer—you often have a tight timeline and limited resources—but done well, your contribution can resonate far and wide. For the Kips Bay Decorator Show House Palm Beach, I was certain that if I didn't go against the grain, I'd be lost in the mix, particularly after being presented with one of the smallest bedrooms in the spacious Mediterranean-style estate. I was determined to avoid the customary vernacular of busy botanical prints and lean into my love of minimalist interiors and sophisticated color palettes. To set the scene, I discovered a Horst P. Horst photograph of 1950s fashion model Jean Patchett in a passionfruit-pink swimsuit staring wistfully off to the distance. The tropical leaf in her hand was our only nod to the home's beachfront address. Around her, I conjured a fairy tale of a Milanese woman, sitting in her bedroom, awaiting the return of her long-lost love. What would that room look like?

From that initial fantasy, we added architecture where there was none, installing fluting on the walls and introducing an innovative curved detail to the ceiling, constructing an atmosphere evocative of Milan's famous landmark Galleria Vittorio Emanuele II, where arched ceilings draw the eye up and play with perspective. These thoughtfully considered elements were tantamount to creating an extraordinary space that seemed to expand beyond its parameters.

Italian design also favors rich natural stones and to include slabs of Breccia Oniciata Rosato marble would indeed be ambitious. Instead, we recreated the look with a man-made material from Cosentino. (As that famous Italian siren Sophia Loren once said, "Sex appeal is fifty percent what you've got, and fifty percent what people think you've got.") With our selection, we fashioned a one-of-a-kind platform bed with undermounted illumination that boosted its ethereal look.

Of course, a Milanese contessa would only have the finest European furnishings, but to push the boundaries of perception, we selected icons of design that sat low to floor, like a voluptuous Gubi chair outfitted in a romantic silk chinoiserie fabric, giving the tiny suite the illusion of height. However, our most formidable challenge to the preconceived rules of scale was reserved for the ceiling, where I employed a massive six-foot chandelier—a precursor to my then-upcoming lighting collection with Studio M—its graceful arms stretching across a graphic wallpaper from my array with Wall&decò. While the circumference of the fixture was certainly a bold choice for a corner suite that measured just thirteen feet by twelve feet, because it had a level of transparency, the chandelier visually lifted the entire room, the cascade of milky orbs strung on raspberry-colored swoops finishing the ensemble like the perfect pair of dangly pearl earrings.

Nothing out of place, perfectly polished, and artfully adorned with an accessory that speaks to one's sense of fashion and individuality: What could be more Milanese than that?

Our bedroom suite for the Kips Bay
Decorator Show House Palm Beach
earned raves for its captivating
interpretation of Milanese glamour,
inspired by this Horst P. Horst
photograph of a swimsuit-clad model
staring longingly off into the distance.

Our studio created a low-lying bed using Dekton Stonika, then added a decadent bolster of S. Harris fabric and Tessitura Fratelli Gargantini linens. Playful vases from Artemest kept with our theme of Italian luxury.

A Wall&decò wallpaper with a tropical
flavor envelops the en suite bath, which we
outfitted with a custom vanity and
pendants from my collection with Studio M.

"WHAT APPEALS TO **THE HEART** GUIDES WHAT INTRIGUES THE MIND; WHAT CHALLENGES THE MIND **MOVES THE BODY.**"

Curvilinear forms are deployed throughout Houston's Gloss Nail Bar,
from the row of oversize seats to the reception area where a
recess on the desk creates an optical illusion with the niche behind.

To give the interior's classic archway a touch of "wow factor," we sculpted
an asymmetrical frame of traditional floral wallpaper that's punctuated with

INSPIRE

Outfitting rooms with
fewer, better things
allows impactful
architectural details
to truly shine.

MANY of the icons I look to for inspiration, like Zaha Hadid, Piero Portaluppi, or Julia Morgan, understood that architecture defines an interior. The precisely executed rectilinear columns of One Thousand Museum in Miami, the spiral staircase of Casa Corbellini-Wassermann in Milan, or the coffered ceilings and arched windows of the Hearst Castle's Celestial Suite in San Simeon, California, establish an atmosphere with just their spatial attributes, not relying on furniture or accoutrements to conjure ambience.

I am more minimalistic in my own practice as well, allowing for the well-executed structure of a space to radiate and inform the aesthetic. That ethos resonated in a unique project on Saadiyat Island in Abu Dhabi, where cultural landmarks like the Louvre Abu Dhabi and Manarat al Saadiyat art center draw a sophisticated crowd of collectors and connoisseurs. My client, a design enthusiast from the royal family, embraced rich colors and sumptuous fabrics, but the waterfront villa she purchased was a white cube. We needed to first transform the blank canvas into a home evocative of the cultural capital with thoughtfully considered dimension.

In the grand entry, we added myriad frames of molding to create a modern interpretation of French boiserie without the fanfare of filigree, the pattern enveloping the space in a visual symmetry that was both arresting and calming. The pattern's synchrony draped down to a majestic landscape of interlocking marble forms stretching throughout the foyer. In the *majlis*, a formal sitting area designed for welcoming guests, a complementary composition of molding pairs with a beautiful wood floor, set in a chevron pattern reminiscent of some of my favorite Haussmann-style apartments.

Implementing natural materials, including expansive slabs of stone, imbued the additions with authenticity. In the living room, a breathtaking accent wall of book-matched green marble created an elegant focal point that harmonizes with the lush natural beauty visible through the adjacent floor-to-ceiling windows. In the kitchen, vertical slabs with veins of honey gold and smoky gray play off cream-colored cabinetry and brass elements.

While the furnishings we brought into this home were all from high-end designers, the pieces whispered luxury without shouting labels. Four regal, crown-shaped lighting fixtures hovered over a pair of armchairs by the Campana Brothers in the foyer. Wondrous de Gournay wallpapers enveloped the main bedroom, bath, and powder room, where an amber glass and marble antoniolupi pedestal sink stands proud between jewelry-like sconces. A Lindsey Adelman ceiling light surmounts a coveted lounge from Ralph Pucci that is suspended near two emerald-green Minotti sofas in the living room.

Having fewer but finer things allowed the beauty of the space to shine through. While an oceanfront villa in Abu Dhabi is far from the proverbial simple life, paring the interior to a few treasured items was simply breathtaking.

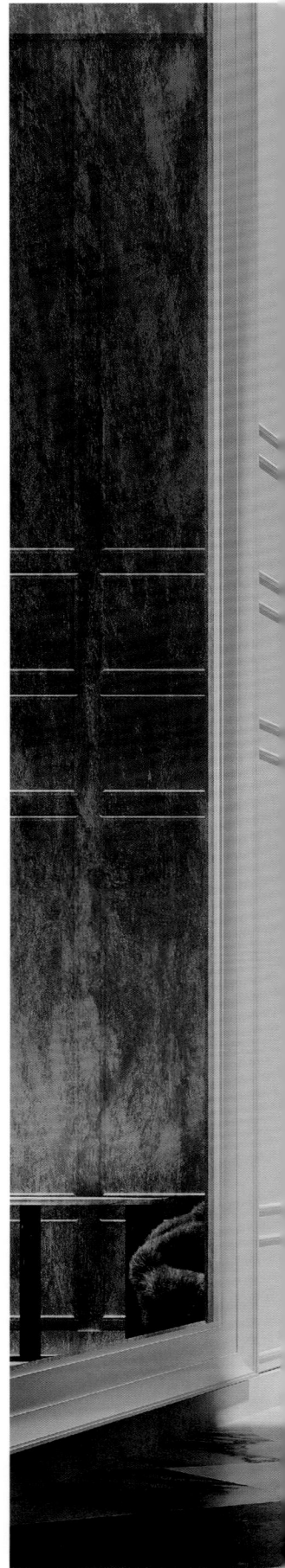

Tropical plantings and warm wood details outside coupled with bold prints and patterns on the interior transformed this modernist home in Abu Dhabi.

A pair of hunter-green Minotti
sofas, a chocolate-colored
Jim Zivic hammock, and contemporary gold-colored chairs by
Knoll take their palette cues from
the book-matched stone slabs
on the living room wall.

An exercise in restrained
elegance, the bath features
a graceful antoniolupi
pedestal washbasin, its
amber bowl echoing the rich
tones of the d'Armes sconces,
de Gournay wallpaper,
and nearby shelves.

A chandelier and trio of pendants composed of pearl-like orbs from Larose Guyon adds a fanciful touch to the dashing kitchen, which is defined by its caramel-colored seating, chevron flooring, and cabinetry.

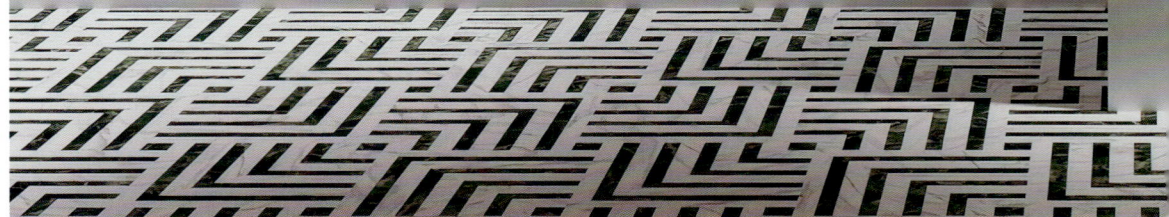

A collection of delicate pendant lights balances the exuberant glamour of the rose-colored de Gournay mural and intoxicating mosaic floor by Kelly Wearstler for Ann Sacks.

A neutral bedroom suite receives a color boost in
the form of a custom, wall-spanning tufted headboard
in our signature shade of peacock green.

Pronounced veins of wispy gray enliven
the snow-white stone that envelops this
tranquil bath, where subtle brass accents
lend the space touches of warmth.

Spherical elements befitting a collector's sculpture garden add visual
interest to the modern home's deftly planted landscape.

"EACH ROOM SHOULD HAVE
AN ELEMENT OF SURPRISE, AN
UNEXPECTED TWIST
IN THE STORY THAT SENDS
THE EXPERIENCE
IN A BEGUILING NEW DIRECTION."

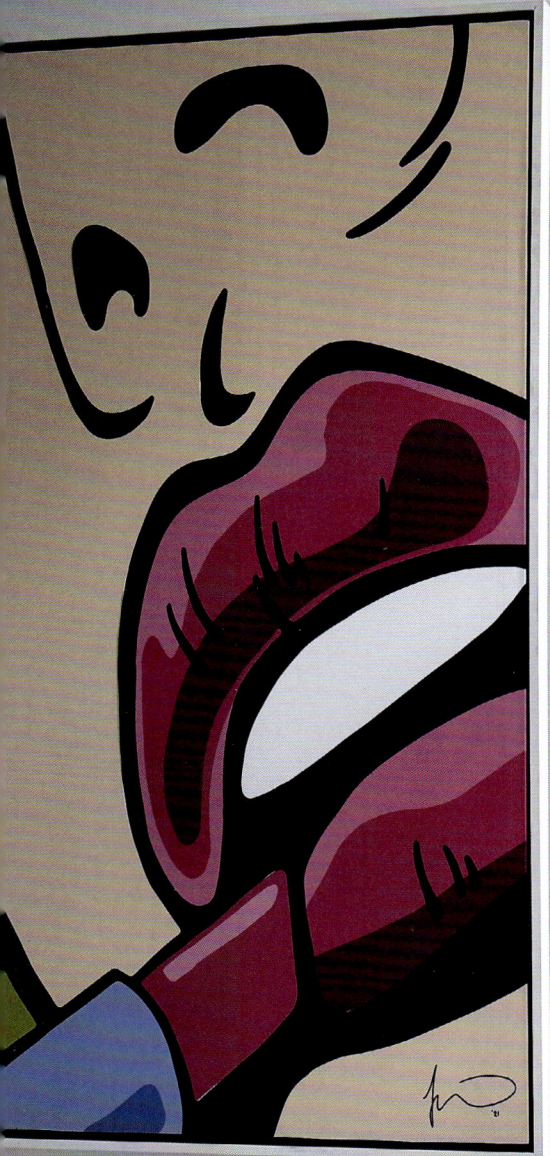

In our FH Residence commission, juxtaposing sleek cooking elements with warm woods transforms a minimalist kitchen into a gourmand's dream with plenty of functional prep area but a decidedly upscale presentation.

A daughter's bath looks youthful but not childlike thanks to the structured pattern of these 3D tiles (their already dramatic effect even more pronounced with the mirror's reflection) and the whimsical suspension lights by Stefano Papi for Slamp.

Suspended over a futuristic-looking Kohler tub,
a Zaha Hadid chandelier gives this otherwise
calming main bath a luminous hint of edge.

ALLURE

A color palette drawn from high fashion is equally captivating in an interior space, electrifying architectural elements and collectible furnishings in sharply contrasting hues.

WHILE

my travels around the globe have greatly influenced my interior design practice, fashion has also been instrumental in shaping my aesthetic. One look I especially love features a palette of black and white, the polar opposites generating a bold visual punch. From Truman Capote's famed Black and White Ball to the striking Aquazzura showrooms in fashion capitals like New York, Miami, and London, the minimalist color plan has stood the test of time and solidified its place as a sartorial mainstay.

So many style-setters have demonstrated the power of the palette, implementing various interpretations to profound effect. Consider Karl Lagerfeld's soigné suiting or Peter Marino's edgy leatherwear—these masters of haute couture readily elevate design with tailoring, embellishments, shape, and texture—not hue.

Interiors often take cues from the runway (and vice versa), so it's hardly shocking to see a room crafted in neutral shades, without the proverbial "pop of color." Shading, texture, and sculptural forms are what then bring the space to life. For a modern home situated in an upscale neighborhood filled with traditional architecture, we leaned into the black-and-white look to really shine a spotlight on this structure's progressive take on the vernacular. In the kitchen, we selected an ebony stone with just a hint of feathery-white veining, polishing the expansive slabs that covered the island and backsplash to a high shine. Then, matte cabinetry, counter stools, and fixtures balance the brightness that's reflected off the glossy cream stone flooring.

Visually compelling elements such as two oversize chandeliers composed of black disks held together on gossamer ebony threads, a structured floating staircase stained in a noirish shade, and a robust entertainment center that incorporates a minimalist fireplace contrast the winter-white walls. Furnishings in soft grays, charcoal, and rich black, including a Roly Poly chair, a towering plinth topped with a sculptural bust, a tufted velvet headboard, and a sinuous, curved sofa punctuate the space with their eye-catching shapes.

Rugs with a tweed-like texture and a feature wall made of large sections of mink-colored fluting bring an elegant coarseness to the home's many smooth surfaces, imbuing the space with depth and dimension. In the stairwell, dynamic pendants in geometric forms with graphic piping hang like modern art. In all, this intoxicating home reverberates with the energy of a sexy New York art gallery, but still welcomes friends and family with warmth and coziness. By balancing light and dark, soft and strong, sleek and textured, we were able to craft an inspired scene that did so much with so little color variation.

Two Luceplan Mesh suspension lamps float above
a collection of Roche Bobois furnishings arranged
on a floor covering from London Grey Rugs.

This home's selection of furnishings was
defined by notable pieces of collectible
design, including a Roly Poly chair
and Spoutnik armchair by Roche Bobois.

Black furniture and materials in various finishes from matte to high shine define the sleek and sexy kitchen.

Small works of art balance the seriousness of the
space, adding touches of whimsy to a sophisticated
grouping of materials and design elements.

A bulbous Roche Bobois Aqua table anchors the
dining area set with the brand's minimalist Aida chairs,
the entire compilation resting upon a textural rug.

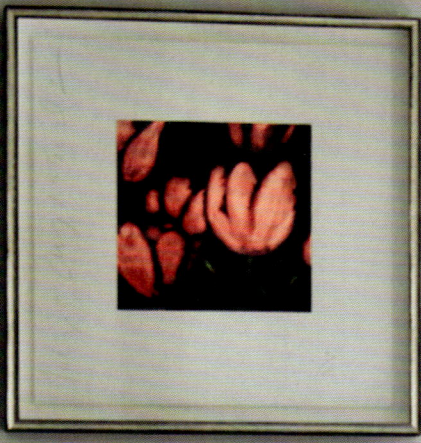

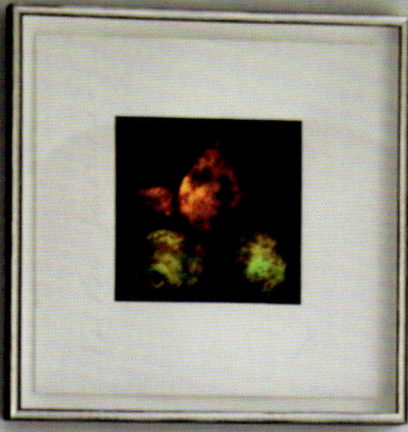

A sinuous sofa reaches
beyond the boundaries
of a circular cocktail table
in a tranquil black, white,
and gray seating area.

A freestanding Kohler tub animates the primary bath,
which is lined in slabs of Porcelanosa stone.

"GLAMOUR IS MORE THAN A PHYSICAL PRESENCE. IT'S AN AURA OF OTHERWORLDLINESS THAT DRAWS ALL IN ITS ORBIT WITH AN IRRESISTIBLE SIREN SONG."

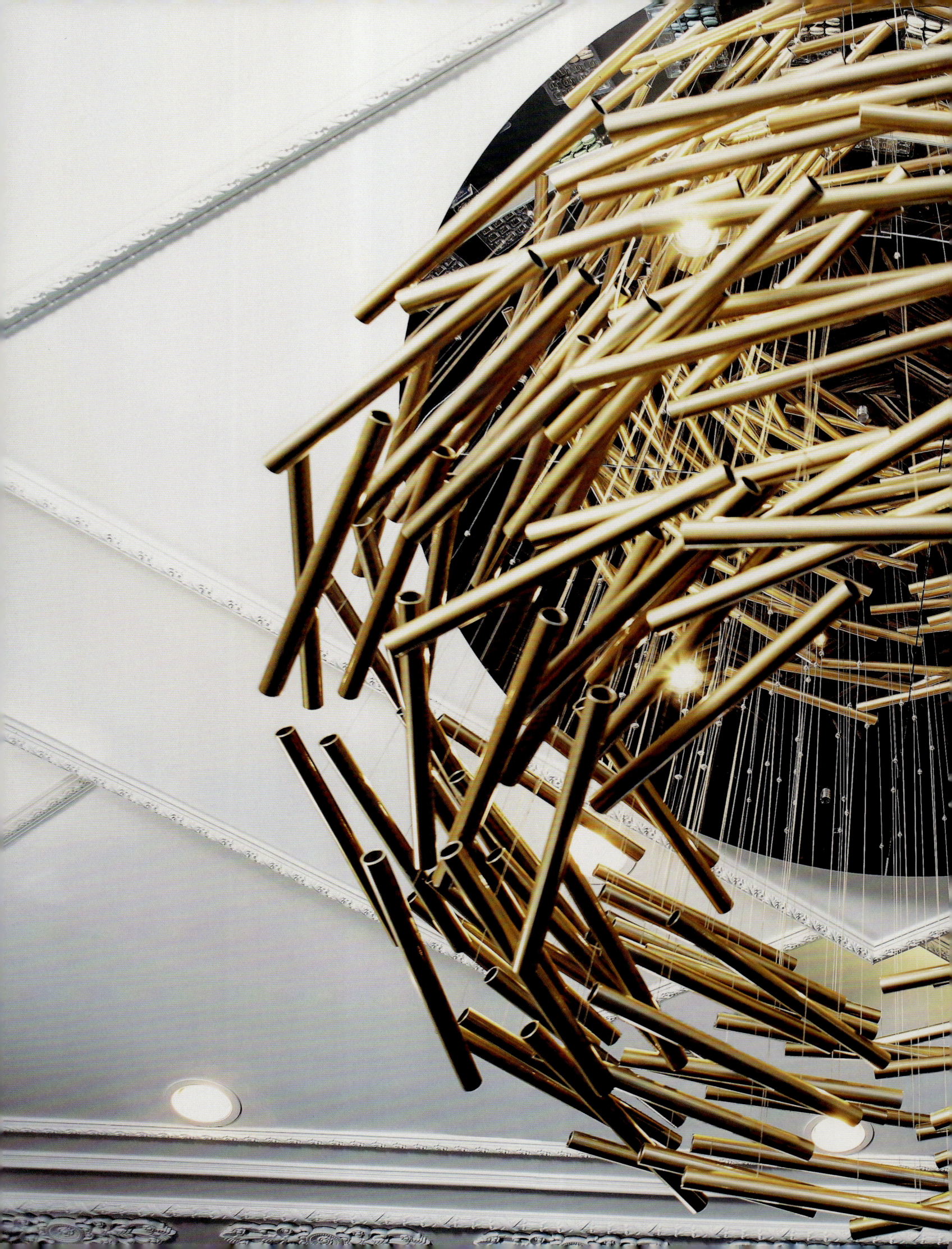

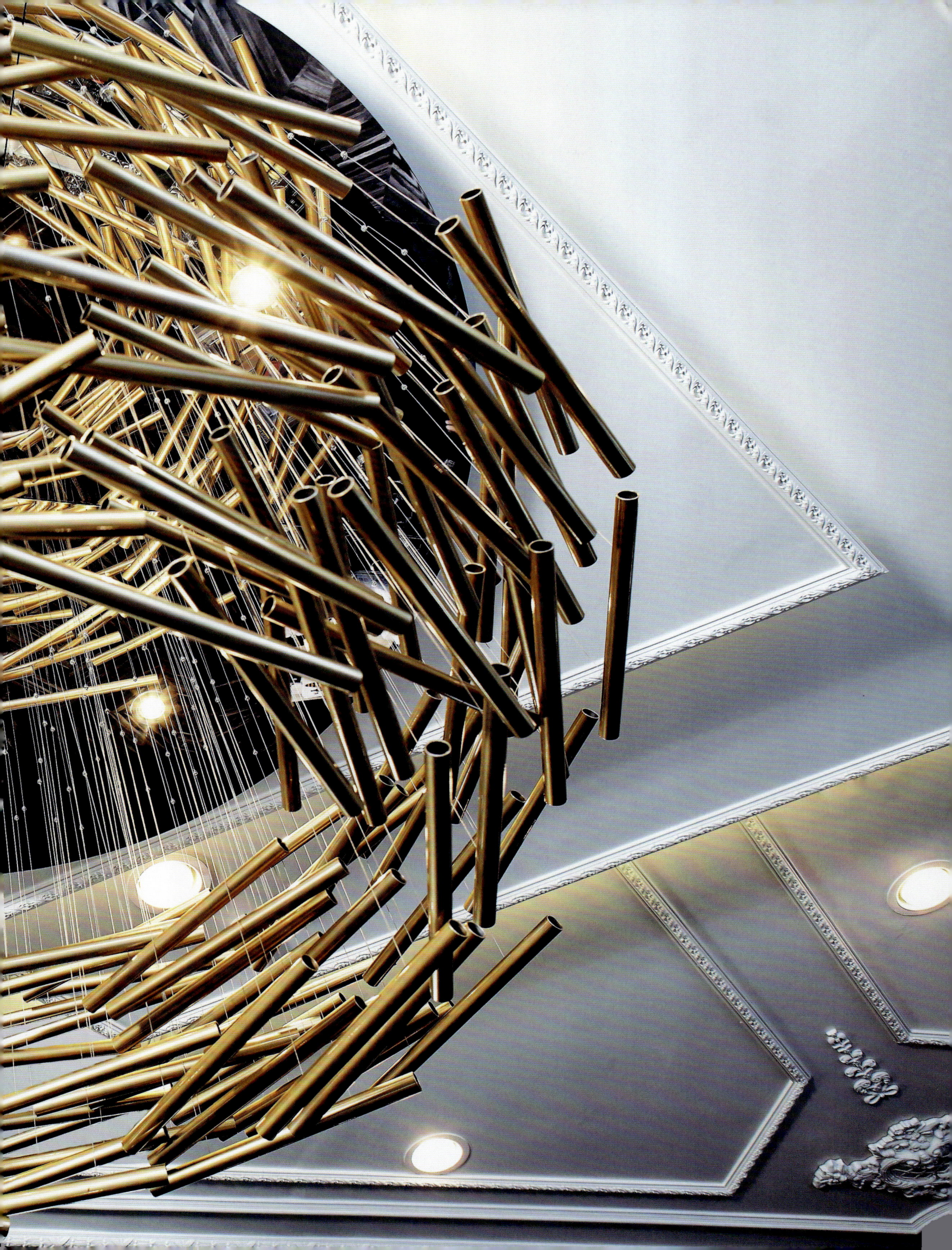

At the Woodlands, Texas, location of Macaron by Patisse, gilt details and a delicate bronze sconce reverberate against jet-black walls that provide a sexy backdrop to glamorous seating in emerald-green velvet.

ENTICE

Balancing high energy with areas of retreat creates captivating living spaces that inspire and rejuvenate.

AS I approached the summation of this book, it motivated me to think about the *why*: Why did each of these clients reach out to an interior designer to shape their spaces? And why me, specifically? As I reflect on each of these projects, I can visualize the blank canvas at the onset and recall the conversations where the homeowners laid bare the sentiment each wanted their interior to evoke. Some were looking to present an air of worldliness and luxury, others tranquility and hospitality. And the fact that we were able to capture those emotions with a compelling blend of architecture, finishes, furnishings, textiles, lighting, and stone is what I love best about this process.

For this modern home, my client, a Houston sportsman, wanted a residence that conveyed his refined taste and requested a design that balanced the sleekness of his contemporary abode with a softer edge that still skewed masculine. Already a collector of modern art, he gravitated to the Miami aesthetic, with its clean white structures and intoxicating energy. To achieve his desired look, we enveloped the rooms in a warm winter white and introduced powerful pops of color, selecting voluptuous dining chairs wrapped in scarlet velvet and structured silver seating with sapphire blue upholstery. These vibrant moments gave the calming interior a touch of verve, bringing life to an otherwise tranquil atmosphere.

With jewel tones, a little can go a long way, and I often gravitate to these saturated shades—emerald greens, ocean blues, and plummy purples routinely finding their way into my work. These deep pigments provide a visual juxtaposition against the more muted neutrals that habitually dominate a modern palette. Atmosphere should ebb and flow—there should be zones that bring serenity and a feeling of retreat while other areas should offer rejuvenation and joie de vivre. It's reflective of how most people use their home: as both a sanctuary and a place to celebrate with others. I have found color to be one of the most effective tools for eliciting those feelings.

That ethos is equally applicable to commercial spaces. Curating showrooms, spas, boutiques, and restaurants, I've used the same guiding force, balancing neutral palettes with punches of gem tones and metallics to bring liveliness into each destination. An overall softness makes visitors feel welcomed, while strategically implementing the bursts of color provides a visual interest without overwhelming, cultivating an experience where it's exciting to arrive and comfortable to linger.

As Coco Chanel once mused, "Fashion changes, but style endures." That guiding principle is what has made Miami—with its art deco buildings and sherbet adornments—a design afficionado's destination. Style is what defined the legacy of grand couturiers like Jean Paul Gaultier and Elsa Schiaparelli. And good taste, something I repeatedly heard I had at the start of my career, remains my touchstone for interiors. I hope, too, that this book has revealed why I am the designer I am today and has inspired you to find your own style.

The circular forms of the Roche Bobois coffee table echo the
soft edges of the Vertigo pendants by Constance Guisset
that float weightlessly over the double-height living room.

The sumptuousness of the Marlow sofa by CasaDesús counterbalances the hard edges of the sleek fireplace and metal accent tables.

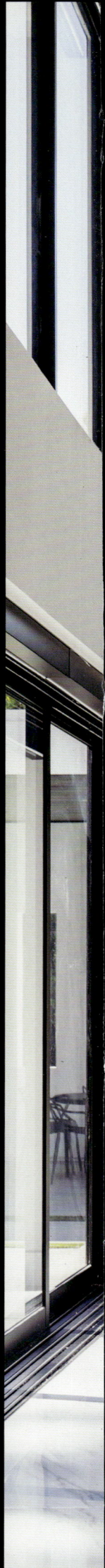

A sculptural Zanotta dining table pairs with the other high-shine elements in the kitchen and dining area, making this a sophisticated but lively area for entertaining guests.

The expansive bath is a picture of serenity
with a sleek freestanding tub set against a tranquil
background of black, white, and gray tones.

"DARKNESS ALLOWS THE IMAGINATION TO STRETCH TO INFINITE BOUNDARIES AND ARRIVE AT A STARRY CONCLUSION WITH LIMITLESS POTENTIAL FOR TRANSFORMATION."

We elevated examples from the Moderno Porcelain Works collection into an immersive art installation inside the company's design gallery, the precise angles of the painterly slabs creating an alluring enfilade that draws visitors further into the space, where a Matisse swivel chair from the Nina Magon Collection for Universal Furniture awaits.

A faceted stone reception
desk matches the angled
forms and neutral tones of the
lounge's soft seating, which
gets a jolt of energy from
a parade of pillows in a
decadent terra-cotta velvet.

Balancing all of the stone are slats of warm
wood that cover a wall and create a visual canopy
over uniquely crafted work areas.

INDULGE

Layering materials of contrasting patterns and textures, and from different periods, brings visual interest to thought-provoking interior spaces.

MANY

forms of design get their boldness from an almost rigid dedication to a singular style. Minimalism and modernism are powerful for their clean lines and lack of ornamentation, just as maximalism and classicism reverberate for their overabundance of stimulation. To me, the most beautiful interiors incorporate a layering of unexpected periods, such as old-world architecture with contemporary furniture elements. Navigating the ruins in Athens, I couldn't help but imagine a B&B Italia sofa juxtaposed against the Temple of Hephaestus or a Roche Bobois chair in conversation with the remarkable carvings found throughout the Acropolis. Surrounded by the Parthenon's towering columns and ornate friezes, I saw it perfectly in my mind's eye as an unbelievable background to the fashion-forward furnishings I often select for my interior designs.

In Ephesus, I stood for hours in a long line to walk through the House of the Virgin Mary, a tiny hut made of ancient stones that opens to a serene garden with a statue of the religious icon. It was powerful to experience the way simple materials and natural elements were brought together to create such a moving environment. On another occasion, I visited a Mediterranean-style resort in Sedona, Arizona, its terra-cotta exterior and tranquil interior of creamy plaster and warm woods providing a captivating opposition to the region's famous red rocks.

For each destination where I've been moved by a neutral palette of organic materials, there are others where I've been awed by color-rich elements transformed into pieces of great beauty. Visiting the mosques in Turkey, I instantly gravitated to the towering columns of pink and purple marble—stones not often seen or utilized in more contemporary design, but I could readily imagine them enveloping the walls of a romantic main bath or creating an eye-catching focal point in a modern kitchen, covering an expansive island with graceful waterfall edges.

For an art-filled home in Beaumont, Texas, I wanted to combine the old and the new, the hard and the soft, to orchestrate a visual mix that spoke to my clients' worldliness and individuality. In the grand living room, two sleek cream-color leather sofas are juxtaposed against a patinated black-brown fireplace surround. The towering walls that define the foyer are stacked with a rugged, earthy stone that's reflected in the high-gloss flooring of soft, silvery gray. Artworks by Pablo Picasso and Andy Warhol that reverberate with a riotous swirl of colors glow in rooms painted winter white and decorated with jet-black furnishings.

Layering can mean so many things in interior design—pattern on pattern, matte against high gloss, a thrilling blend of rugged and refined textiles, hard edges paired with sinuous shapes. But, when accurately executed, the thoughtful mix creates a space that offers visually arresting vignettes from every viewpoint and tantalizes the imagination at every turn.

The soaring entry balances rough stone walls with contemporary elements, like high-gloss flooring, a custom leather bench, and dynamic artwork by Robert Kushner.

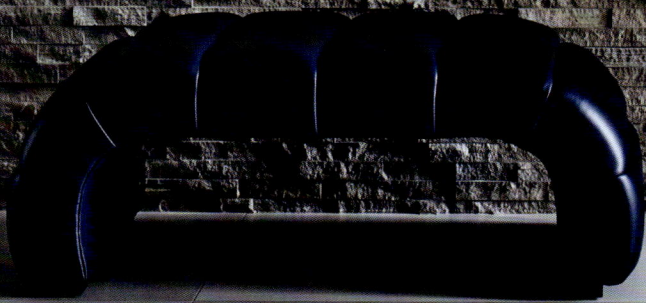

Art complements every room of this collector's residence, including
the kitchen where the canvas's strokes of tangerine reverberate
in a space defined by elements of black, brown, and white.

Multidimensional works, such as the intense
John Keane painting, right, bring life to a quiet hallway
that's completely enveloped in smoky gray hues.

A Kohler tub stands almost like a sculpture against an eye-catching
floor-to-ceiling installation of linear Porcelanosa tile.

"MOTHER NATURE CONJURES THE MAGNIFICENT COLORS AND DIVERSE TEXTURES THAT LURE US OUTSIDE AND INSPIRE US TO IMAGINE THEIR POSSIBILITIES ON THE CANVAS THAT IS OUR INTERIOR SPACES.

A backlit onyx wall and black stone sink add
opulence to a contemporary home outside Houston,
Texas, defined by its mix of elevated materials.

Metal shelves float above a pair of Pierre Jeanneret–inspired chairs in a home office that includes a minimalist B&B Italia marble table and custom rug.

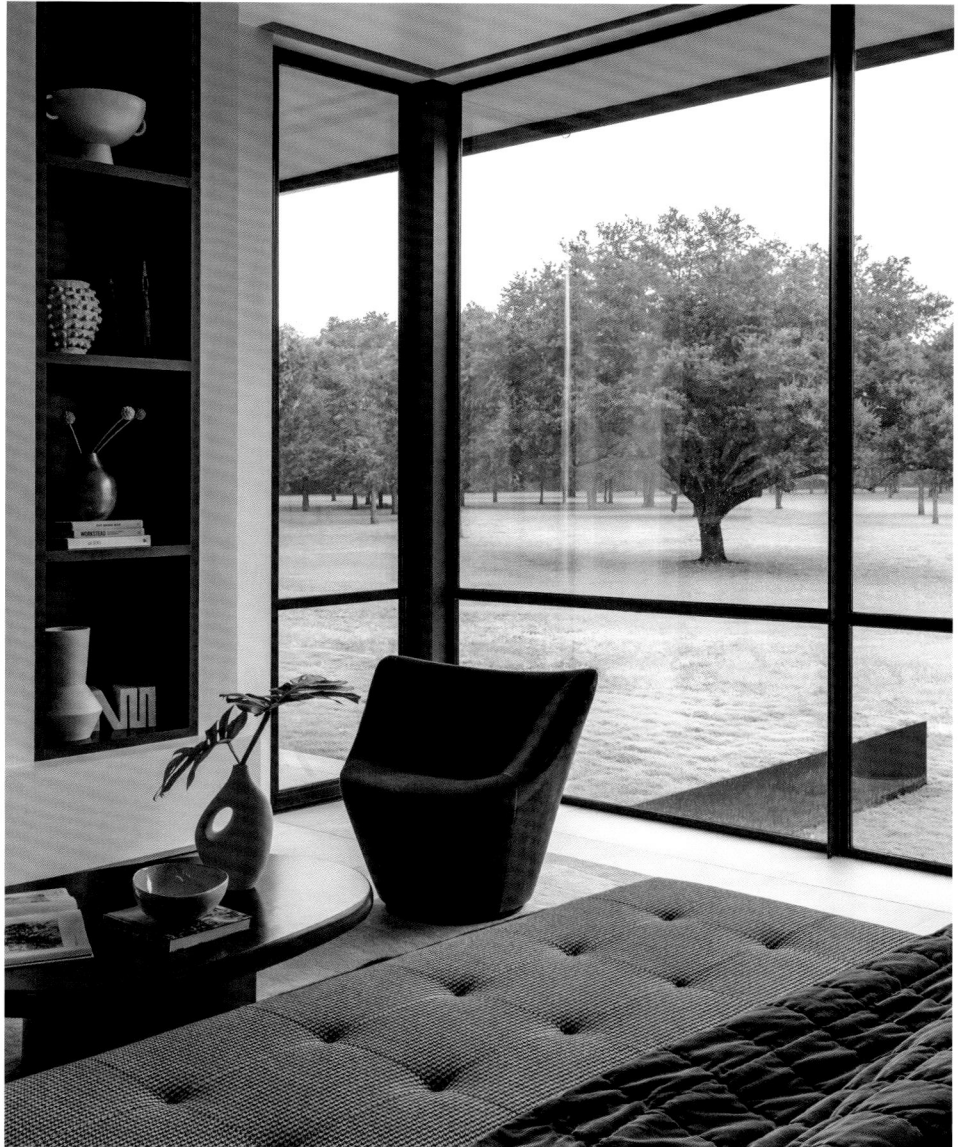

Custom furnishings paired with design icons such as Pierre Paulin's
Anda armchairs from Ligne Roset and the fluttery 21 Series
Multi-Light pendant by Bocci cultivate a restful and inspiring main
suite ideal for both relaxation and rejuvenation.

Thoughtful sight lines distinguish this masterfully conceived
modern residence most notably in this secluded lounge area tucked
behind a double-sided fireplace in the primary bedroom.

In the main bath, a custom concrete tub situated atop a river rock–style stone flooring connects to the exterior materials viewed through the floor-to-ceiling glass windows.

The exterior's slatted stained wood ceiling contrasts with the more neutral materials in the living room, where an ivory Molteni&C sectional wraps around a sculptural resin coffee table by Olivya Stone. A gunmetal-gray Cassina chair with contrasting stitching nods to the bespoke light fixture by Yellow Goat Design.

An elegantly restrained fireplace anchors one end of the living room while a fantasy wine room dominates the other.

The textural design of the
linear porcelain backsplash
draws the eye to this
minimalist Poggenpohl
kitchen, in which Marco
Zito black leather barstools
surround an architectural
island that balances
matte countertops and
high-gloss cabinetry.

A collection of mustard-yellow
dining chairs adds a jolt of energy to
the monochromatic eat-in kitchen.

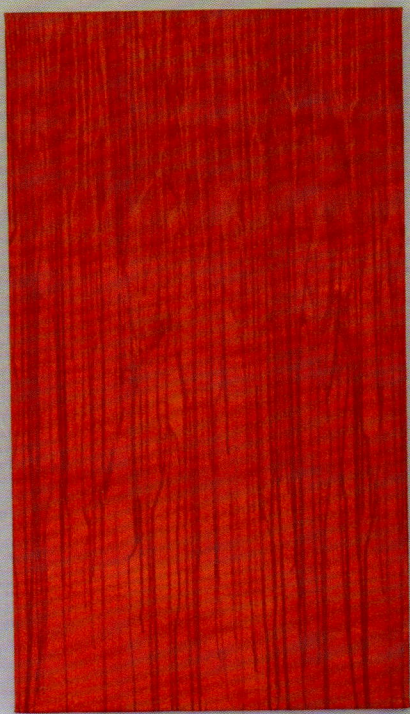

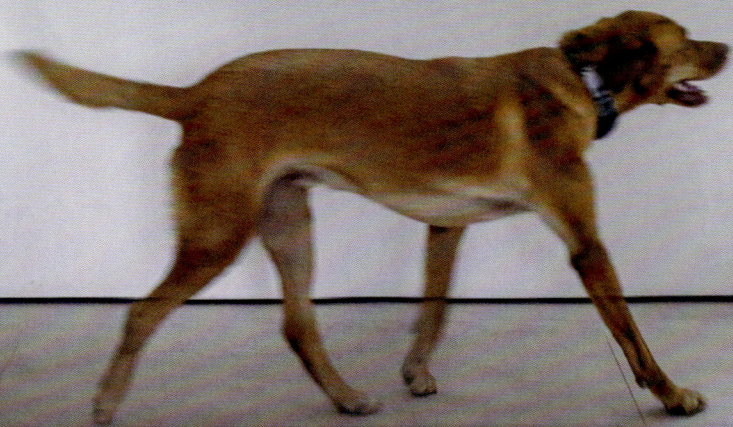

A fiery canvas electrifies an otherwise neutral passageway.

Hard and soft collectible contemporary furnishings animate
a family-friendly playroom, where a velvety Ligne Roset
Togo sofa is paired with a mesmerizing Glas Italia side table

A low-profile platform bed, dressed in rich olive and sapphire-color linens, rests in front of a custom wood wall installation in a guest suite.

A skylight floods the guest bath with natural
light and gives the masculine space
the aura of a decadent outdoor shower.

Visible wood grain and stone veining enliven an otherwise restful bedroom, outfitted with a custom rug and whimsical Roly Poly chair, and bathroom sanctuary that hosts an eye-catching Kohler soaking tub and streamlined sconces from Roll & Hill.

Low-lying RH furniture is installed on the terrace, the wood details of the chaises echoing the wood pattern on the ceiling above. Multiple rooms featured floor-to-ceiling windows allowing for an unimpeded view of the exterior architecture and bucolic landscape.

ACKNOWLEDGMENTS

This book was first and foremost made possible by the grace of God, and the unwavering support of Karun, Aryan, and Alina Magon.

Thank you to my loving parents, Dr. Arun Verma and Mrs. Vinni Verma, for instilling in me a never-ending drive to succeed.

I would like to express my deep gratitude to Monacelli for providing me with a platform to publish my design point of view, to Christina Juarez for believing in me and my design aesthetic, to Doug Turshen and Steve Turner for making my dreams come true, and to Jill Sieracki for expressing my voice and emotions so eloquently.

Thank you to Adrian Duenas and Marcello Saenz for the continuous love and support, and to Patty Dominguez, Eduardo Cosentino, and the entire Cosentino family, Nathan and Naomi Sperling and my Studio M team, Sahrai Milano, Universal Furniture, Product Lounge, and Wall&decò for their steadfast belief in me and my abilities.

Thanks to Jay Marroquin, Dennis Clendennen, and Lisa Pelayo for bringing their creative visions to life through my portraits, and to all the photographers who were involved in these projects.

Thanks to my right hands, Tanner Doggett and Nataly Montoya, and my entire Nina Magon Studio family for their undying support and love.

Thank you to Dolce & Gabbana, Balmain, Christian Siriano, and Saint Laurent for the most outstanding outfits.

Most importantly, thank you to all of our wonderful clients and my close family and friends who have supported me unconditionally, which has resulted in the creation of this publication.